PAY
DAY

Interactive Multimedia Created by Carole & Michael Marsh

THE GRAND CANYON: Mother-of-all-Holes-in-the-Ground!

KABOOM!: VOLCANOES, Mountains With a Tummyache

"The Mushroom on Mars Hill!": THE WORLD FAMOUS LOWELL OBSERVATORY, Flagstaff, Arizona

DEATH VALLEY, California & The Secret of Scotty's Castle!

THE (Phantastic!) PAINTED DESERT & THE (Phenomenal!) PETRIFIED FOREST

THE AMERICAN INDIAN DICTIONARY FOR KIDS, Featuring all 50 States!

"Branching Out!":
BIG TREES OF THE WORLD

LOUISVILLE, KENTUCKY: Home of the World Famous Kentucky Derby, "the Most Exciting Two Minutes in Sports!"!

ALLIGATORS & CROCODILES:
"The Tooth, the Whole Tooth & Nothing But the Tooth!"

BEACHY KEEN!:
Everything About Beaches for Kids

Other HOW TO MAKE A MILLION BOOKS by Carole Marsh

How To Make a Million Writing for Kids!

How To Make a Million Publishing Yourself!

How To Make a Million From Home!

And new for January 1, 1995:

How to Make a Million Creating & Developing Multimedia: A Practical Primer for Publishers & Others

JOIN US!

From the "HOW TO MAKE A MILLION" SERIES . . .

Gallopade!

The World's Largest Publishing Company Presents . .

How to Make a Million Writing For the New Interactive Multimedia & CD-ROM Market!

by Carole Marsh,
Founder, Carole Marsh
Family Interactive
Multimedia &
CD-ROM

For information, contact Gallopade!,
The World's Largest Publishing Company,
359 Milledge Ave., Suite 100,
Atlanta, Georgia 30312,
1-800-536-2GET

Book design by Michael Marsh

ISBN: 0-7933-7624-6

For Bob, Michele & Michael,
my multimedia, multi-everything team!

Contents

PART 1: "Let's Interact!"

PART II: How to Write for Multimedia

Part I:

"Let's Interact!"

Chapter One:

Why Should You Listen to Me?

Like any new industry (especially as complex, ethereal & futuristic as multimedia!), there are plenty of come-ons, promises, deceptions & worse. *Why should you listen to me?*

Because I've done it! Not the million $ part yet — I'm still working on that. But I have written 10 interactive multimedia programs that are now selling quite well, thanks very much, all around the United States via my own direct mail campaign to schools & public libraries + through the efforts of outside distributors.

Was it easy to get started in multimedia? No, because I didn't have a book like this to show me where "start" was! *Did it take a lot longer than I expected?* Yes. *Did it cost a lot to get into multimedia?* Yes & no. *Was it worth it?* Exceedingly so! *Am I done now?* No, I've only just scratched the surface. *Is it fun?* You bet. *Is it easy?* In some ways, very, but it requires a new kind of thinking & creativity. *Is it lucrative?* So far, so good, & I believe the long term prospects are tremendous! *Am I trying tobe encouraging?* YES! *Do I think the time is right for you to get involved?* Absolutely perfect! *What do you need?* Nothing except your enthusiasm, energy, patience, time, skills & best efforts.

My goal with this short, simple book is to get you started off on the right foot. To share the type of critical & practical information I was unable to obtain when I got started. To help you see your potential in this exciting new industry, especially how you can apply your writing talents, current manuscripts & future marketing efforts as you pursue the hot new field of multimedia. As a recent industry article said, *"This is gonna be what pays our pensions."*

Let's get started!

Carole Marsh

My goal with this Smart, simple book is to get you started off on the right foot. [illegible]

[illegible]

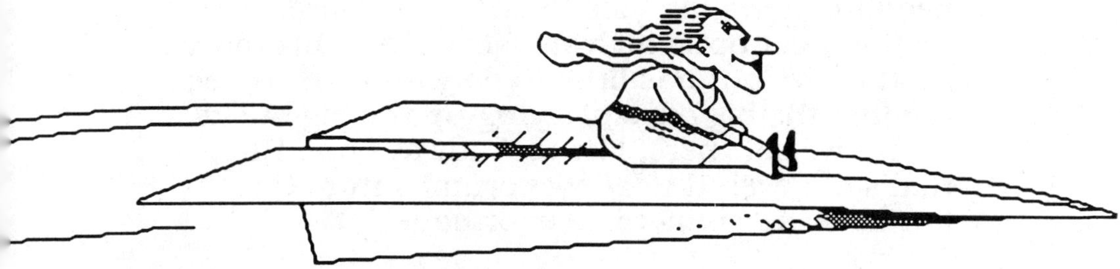

Chapter Two:

Let Me Bring You Up to Speed!

Multimedia has existed for a long time. Many people were working in this industry even before it began to have fancy new names like interactive, multimedia & CD-ROM. The good news is that they've done all the preliminary, expensive, truly difficult work for us!

Right now, as you know, multimedia is headline news *ala* Vice President Al Gore, virtual reality, fiber optic highways & such. This too is good news, but has little to do with you. These are just the big guys divvying up the big bucks before we get there, like they always do. But that's ok; even the *leftover* crumbs from this industry are going to be enormous!

Yes, some folks are already way ahead of you. Some are light speed ahead, but they're just the pioneers for the next generation of multimedia, so ignore them for now. Others actually have products on sale & in use. There're already interactive encyclopedias, interactive storybooks, Shakespeare & the CIA in multimedia formats. There're also lots of games & plenty of super simple stuff like learning to add & subtract programs.
But programs get more creative every day!

In my opinion, the main folks who've had a crack at multimedia so far are computer people. Yes, they sure have a head start on most writers when it comes to complex computer issues. But because they may lack creativity, skill & experience (in writing areas) & own little or no content (meaning a lot of what they've developed someone else wrote or is from the public domain), it's beginning to be *our* time to shine!

This is the *perfect* time to get into multimedia! There's finally beginning to be a big enough base market so you can make, instead of lose, money. A lot of truly difficult problems have been worked out, though plenty of bugs remain. Users are beginning to look for diverse products, both practical & escapist — just as they do from books. And although games are still popular, consumers are now seeking value, purpose, & solutions to entice them to continue to invest in multimedia.

NOTES

In an early critique of this book in the *Washington Post,* reporter Don Oldenburg astutely commented that I did not quite tell readers exactly how much money they could expect to make for writing a multimedia program. The reasons it is difficult to be specific are wonderful omens for writers everywhere!

The truth is YOU will say how much your talents are worth, & it's about time. If you read this book & do a prototype program, you'll get the best feel of how much time it might take to complete a project (+coordination with other team members, checking proof disks, etc.) Because you'll be providing an expertise that's high-tech & on the cutting edge, you should be able to command a fine fee for your work, but only YOU can say what that is.

On the other end of the spectrum, getting your foot in the door is often worth providing your services for a reasonable fee, even free! The size of the project, publisher, budget, etc. all impact on the price for your services that the market will bear. There is no wrong amount.

II. Software

The same goes for the development software used to create a multimedia program. Generally, if you author it for Macintosh, it won't run on IBM & vice versa. But these barriers are slowly falling. It'll take a while longer for it to be cheap & easy for you to do a joint program, but that's no reason for you to wait. Get started *in some format* & you'll be a lot more ready for the next step than the writer who waited for a perfect starting time.

III. CD-ROM

The Compact Disk-Read Only Memory (you know, the little shiny, silver platter) is solving lots of the previously-mentioned problems. Just as you saw in the music industry, where now any audio CD will play in any player, the same will eventually happen with CD-ROM. Why? Because it's in everybody's $elf intere$t!

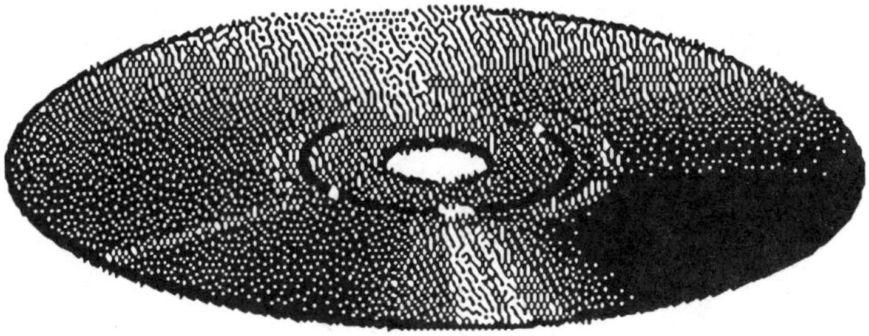

IV. Compatibility

"Compatibility" (or perhaps the lack of it) is the main stumbling block in multimedia right now. For a while, everyone had to worry about High Sierra, ISO this, Red Book that. The folks trying to figure it all out still do, but you don't. The standard that seems to be the final winner is ISO 9660. Who knows what this means? *Who cares!* Like an end-user, all we want is to be able to write for multimedia like we write for a book. And then, let simple software do its thing to convert it into a medium (probably CD-ROM) that runs on most any machine around the world. This dream is coming closer & closer to reality everyday!

Chapter Four:

A Word of Encouragement

If you're a writer, you're a *natural* for multimedia! And why not? Your world to-date has been creativity, visualization, communication, research, accuracy, emotion, details & joy! These are *exactly* the skills & tools required for successful multimedia authoring & products. So don't worry so much about the technical end & do what *you* do best — write.

If you're an author & own copyrights, you're in the catbird seat! *Content* is what is lacking. The first items to have been multimediaed have either been basic reference tools such as the encyclopedia or literary classics like Shakespeare's plays & *Peter Rabbit.* If you have material you're entitled to convert to multimedia, you can begin today, or, create new work from scratch, just for multimedia.

Publishers, I know this is difficult for you. How do I know? Because I'm a publisher too. For the record, I don't believe the book is going anywhere either. (At least not while *we're* around.) But I have exhibited books this year + set up a single multimedia station. Less than 1% of adults made a beeline to the multimedia computer; they had to be wooed there. BUT, virtually 100% of any kids age 6-16 ignored the books & immediately latched onto the mouse (whether they'd used one before or not!) & pointed & clicked their way through the programs, often having to be dragged away by their parents. And note: these are educational programs — not games! They are virtually my *books* in multimedia format.

Yes, we publishers will find this new challenge difficult, time consuming & expensive. But it's unavoidable. Actually, I think we're exceedingly well prepared for multimedia, will find it easier (thank goodness!) than the trauma of going from typewriters to computers, & will excel in it because our hearts are in the right place (communication with the customer) & our talents & contacts extensive & deep, especially our associations with writers. Computer people (in-house or service bureaus) can do the rest.

Contact your writers now; encourage them to consider this alternative to the "book." Perhaps a dual book/multimedia product will help get your feet wet? There's money to be made. And multimedia's really just a *very special* book!

NOTES

This is an optimum time for progressive writers willing to keep up with the times, learn new skills & provide exceedingly creative talent to a project to also grow up in how they get paid. Each assignment will be different. You could get paid by the hour, the project, an advance & royalties, or, consider receiving a fee for your part of the project + residuals (or whatever they will be called) or some other "piece of the action" from future sales. As some book publishers lobby for reducing traditional royalties from 10% to 5%, what have you got to lose by being more flexible about payment options, especially if you may actually net more dollars over the long run of the product's sales?

Chapter Five:

The Right Write Stuff About Multimedia

Ok, writer, now that you have a brief overview of the industry & opportunity as they stand today, let's be "interactive" — <u>you</u> ask the questions!:

1. *What's the <u>same</u> about writing for a book & writing for multimedia?*

The **audience** is the same!: Like always, you'll be writing for as specific an audience as possible. You'll still communicate in the same way with the same words. (What a relief, hey?!)

Your **objective** will still be the same: Want to educate them? Make them abstain from sex? Make them hungry for chocolate? Help them learn to build a sailboat? Make them laugh & cry at the same time? You can still achieve your same goals with multimedia — maybe even more so!

2. What is different about writing for multimedia than writing an article, manual, book, etc.?

I'm so glad you asked! The difference is a little hard to explain. It's a list. A combination of things. Some of these include:

- Multimedia is very **multi-dimensional**. I describe it as the difference between playing regular chess & 3-dimensional chess. It's the same, but different. Needless to say, it requires you to maintain an intense concentration, be very organized, know what you're talking (writing) about & remember your audience & objective so you can build the multimedia communication they need. But, what's so different about writing a book? Not much, & yet, everything!

- Multimedia is more **visceral**. When I first started writing multimedia programs, I thought it was fun to be able to "link" [we'll get to these definitions in a minute, but note, if this were a multimedia program, you could "click" on that new term & be taken directly ("linked") to its definition, then easily return to where you left off] a paragraph of type with a piece of animation that demonstrated what I was trying to explain. But the day I really got angry because I could write about the ocean, show the ocean in motion, let the reader (user) hear the ocean BUT couldn't let them smell & taste the salt air, I knew I was hooked on multimedia! In spite of all its new abilities to communicate, I wanted it to do more. I discovered I was not only able to communicate & share with my reader in some exciting new ways, but that that only made me want to open the door wider.

Why *couldn't* they get their feet wet?! (I understand smell & touch are on the way, but you have enough to cope with right now.)

Multimedia, in my opinion, is more (& less) helpful to the user than a book. Obviously, if I'm only interested in quotations by cannibals about lunch, then it's quick & easy "find" that randomly strewn information in a document with the aid of a search process. And if I'm a dinosaur-crazy kid, what fun to poke around a program & only look at & read & see & listen to the things that interest me, like big teeth & loud roars! But if I'm the *writer*, I organize my material (like this book for example) in the way I think will be most helpful to the reader. This vertical way (scrolling down my computer screen) is how I wrote it. This horizontal way (turning pages) is how I expect you to read it. But if this book is mutimediarized, then you can "read" it in an an almost endless array of "directions." This option, to me, is one of the most "different" things about multimedia. It has its good points, & its bad. Of course, a reader could always read the index of a book, then the table of contents, then chapter six. But that's not how we usually read a book. But it is how multimedia users will "read" a program. Hopefully, they'll find our intentional organization helpful & not go off on random chases of tyrannosaurus rexes & perhaps never even discover the 18-inch prehistoric cockroaches you document. But that is their option & it's your job to make all these exciting new ways to not just "read," but "experience" a book easy & beneficial to them.

 Multimedia is a little factoid-ish, sound-biteish to me. Because a user sees the "book" on a screen, they only see a little bit of the entire product at a time. Yes, this should seem like a "page," but it doesn't. Again, it will be your job to lure the user into the entire "book," using stuff you're good at, writer: cues, hints, tips & (graphic artists!) art, color, texture, & (photographers!) pictures, & (audiographers!) sound, & (videographers) motion.

All this means that, you, the writer, will become a little more of an *orchestrator*. You may not have to do a single technical thing to create a multimedia program, but you will have to be aware of the bits & pieces it takes to make a program if you want to do the best writing job. (Perhaps scriptwriters should have a slight edge in this new medium?)

Multimedia is not a book; but, it is not not a book. So far, I've written my initial multimedia drafts just as if they were going to be a book. (In fact, what I also ended up with were interactive books, which are now on the market!) I was surprised at how few adaptations I had to make to accommodate multimedia . . . and, how many. I ended up with all the information that was in my book, but I did not end up with a book. How different does that make multimedia writing from regular writing? You'll soon see! How does that make a "book" on a computer screen or television monitor different from a cloth or paperback book? We're all waiting for the customer to say. So far, the main difference I've found is that a book sits on your tummy so much nicer in a hammock than a big heavy computer!

Multimedia is hard to proof!: If you thought proofing *Gone With the Wind* was a chore, try proofing a program that can be "read" a myriad of ways.

NOTES

I advise you to "invite yourself" to the multimedia party, because currently, computer types are multimediaing without you! But I also suggest you invite yourself to participate in appropriate financial rewards for your services. Be fair, be reasonable, but don't be tentative. If you establish a good reputation, outstanding product credentials & super professionalism, your services should be in high demand.

But just how much multimedia moola does that equal an hour? Fill-in-the-blank yourself!

Chapter Six:

Multimedia Glossary!

Oh, so this is multimedia — I'm gonna move the glossary that every writer knows perfectly well belongs at the end of the book to page 46! But if I don't tell you these few terms right here & now, you'll be stumped for the next section of the book. This list is short & sweet, but it's all you really need to know to get started writing multimedia.

CARD or SCREEN: the individual window of information your reader/user will see at 1 time. I equate this to a *paragraph* IF your basic text typesize is going to be 14 point or more (for younger readers, for example) or a *page*, if you'll have the Gettysburg Address on a single screen, for example. Cards/screens can be scrolled, so can be as long as you wish.

BUTTON: a word, picture, card, *anything* that the user can "click on" & be whisked to a new screen of information (whether that's a picture, video, etc.) Most of the time, a button is made obvious by being a **bold word**, an icon or some other cue (like CLICK HERE.)

HOT: a button is "hot" if you can click on it & something happens. You might see a user "click on" on various items on the screen (words, pictures) to see if they're "hot," so help out by making **hot** buttons obvious, since not all picture items will be hot.

CLICK ON: When you take your cursor & put it on an item & use your mouse or joystick or key to select it & activate it to do what it's gonna do, usually open, close or change something.

LINK: a link can be the card or picture or video or animation, etc. that clicking on a button takes you to. A link is really a script (often accomplished without doing any scripting at all, since you can use pre-scripted buttons) that causes the button to do its thing, such as "link" the user from a word to its definition. i. e., 1 card to another.

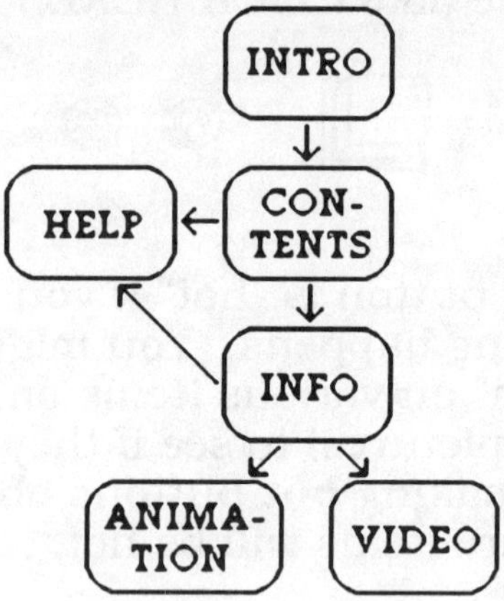

STACK: linked cards; usually are of similar information, such as biographies, for example; can have the same borders, art, etc., so that you can just "copy" a card & add new information to it.

Words you don't need to know to write multimedia right now:

Multiplatform: 1 disk that will run on different type computers
Multilingual: a program that can be run in more than 1 language
Authoring software: an application that sets up the program to be read onto a disk; the writer DOES NOT have to write in this
Retrieval software: an application the user needs to run the program on their computer
Compression: reducing the final program to take up less memory
Premastering: getting a program ready for CD-ROM replication
One-off: a premastered CD-ROM; used for final checks
Replication: the "printing" or impressing of CD-ROM disks
CD-I (CD-Interactive),
CD-XA (CD Extended Architecture),
CDTV (a Commodore product);
all = proprietary software/hardware

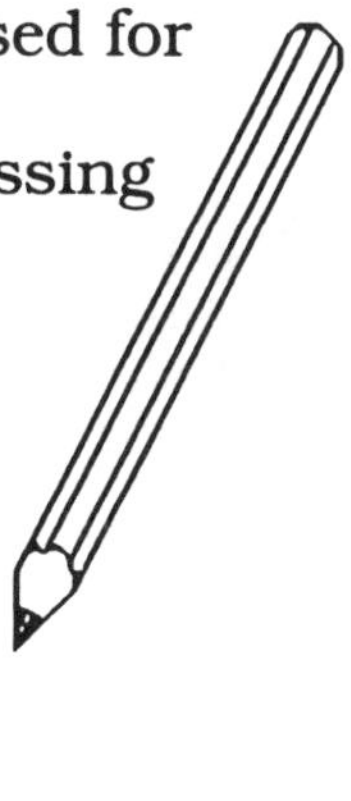

NOTES

ZCI is the first publisher I've seen actually advertise for multimedia writers. They are currently looking for "knowledgeable authors" to help create "directed learning" multimedia titles. You should be an "expert" on a subject to apply & work with a Windows environment. If you qualify, contact ZCI Publishing, Infomart, 1950 Stemmons, Ste. 6048, Dallas, TX 75207.

Part II:

How to Write for Multimedia

Chapter Seven:

Getting Started

Now I hope you won't hold it against me that I'm keeping this as elementary as possible. You may be a lot smarter than me, but when I first started writing multimedia, I read a whole lot of confusing books that were supposed to be "basic" & "beginner" but never, as near as I could tell, told me exactly what to do & when & how. I hope I do a better job than they did, even if it means erring on the side of Simple Simon.

WHAT YOU WILL NEED:

Your current computer & word processing program. Just like a book, until you get a good manuscript, there's nothing to do but organize your work & write. (I told you this was going to be easy!)

Note: The assumption this book makes is that you're going to write a short interactive multimedia program on a tightly-focused topic. It's a good way to start.

GETTING READY:

Or, this is just like writing a book!

1. *Select your topic.* Because multimedia offers the opportunity for more than words & illustrations to communicate, you may want to keep your focus a little narrower than usual. For example, a multimedia program on dinosaurs could run for an endless number of pages, require all kinds of art, allow for all types of animation, sound effects, photographs & video. In other words, your book will be "bigger" than normal. Because sights & sounds will also help "tell" your story, you may find your writing job is a little bit easier.

TIP: A note about "big." Some folks assume that because multimedia formats allow for a lot of room (memory), the more information, the merrier. This may be true of a national telephone directory, a parts manual or the complete works of Shakespeare. But more is not necessarily better if your user, sooner rather than later, wants to get around to all the info in the program so they'll know how to tie-dye a tee shirt, for example. You can still get in the history of tie-dying, etc., but 5,000 pages on tie-dying (just because you have unlimited space) may be overkill?

2. *Target your audience:* Just as audience selection dictates the number of pages, type of language, reading level, inclusion or exclusion of certain information, addition of a glossary or other preface or end material for a book, the same will be true for multimedia.

3. *Do your research:* We're still in book city, aren't we! And yet, with multimedia EVEN IF YOU ONLY DO THE WRITING, it will be beneficial to all if you have some knowledge of the types of illustration, photos, animation, sound effects, video, etc. that may be used in the program. Since much of this may come directly from your research material, you might want to note appropriate (often even critical) visuals that could/should be used.

4. *Write a title:* Because the user cannot "flip thru" a shrink-wrapped multimedia program like they can a book, your title needs to be as communicative as possible about the content & market for the program.

5. *Outline your work:* If you don't outline, that's ok. If you do, you may find that you make adjustments to your way of outlining after you do your first multimedia program. But for now, your basic outline of introductions, chapters, appendices, etc. is perfectly logical.

6. *Make a table of contents & a list of STACKS:* the contents list will define the major areas of the program; the stacks represent the different types of information you'll include: bios, maps, graphs, definitions, activities, stories, history, for examples.

Writers!

URGENT RESEARCH TIP!: It will be very helpful if you have all the research you plan to use assembled around you when you begin to write. Why? Because *variety* is the spice of multimedia. If you plan to write & link at the same time (which I advise), then you will need the information at your fingertips for quotations, glossary definitions, geographic descriptions, biographies, etc. (or whatever <u>your</u> program categories are). One nice thing about writing for multimedia is that there seems to be a comfortable home for the entertaining "asides" such as trivia, even recipes, etc., that may be more awkward to incorporate in a book. If you try to write your cards separately & then link them, you'll want to check-off what info you've used. Believe me, 1,000 cards later, things can get pretty confusing if you're not organized!

Chapter Eight:

A Quick Look at Some Programs Before You Begin to Write!

Well, actually I'm not going to show you any. This is a book after all, so even now you begin to see some of the benefits of multi-media — if this was an interactive program, I'd just insert a hot button here for you to click on & go to a video of an example of multimedia!

When I first began to write for multi-media, my goal was NOT to see what others had done! Being an ultra-creative soul, I wanted to invent that wheel for myself. And what did I end up with?

Well, being very reader-oriented, I made the assumption that they were probably as confused as I was about the new media. Also, I hate seeing an icon that looks great (artwise), but means nothing (communicationwise) & the computer person is "too cool" to do anything as unmultimedia mundane as put words under it so that I will know whether it means STOP, YIELD, GO DIRECTLY TO GO, GLOSSARY, VISUAL, BIBLIOGRAPHY, HOT DOG or whatever.

So, I created a very simple, user-friendly, book motif, plain-English, interactive multimedia program that I was soon very comfortable using & that users navigated around readily & had virtually no questions about most anything they "clicked on."

True, there were fewer bells & whistles than multimedia I later saw when I finally got brave enough to take a look & see how good or bad I had done in my dark ignorance.

What I discovered I'd created was a **master** that was a comfortable jump from book to computer program & that made **writing** the star, & sound effects & visuals enhancements. I was pleased. It was a good start. It suited me. It suited my customer. And I had a base to work from that I understood.

As time has gone by, I've marveled at all I was able to put into those original programs. They had all the oomph, pizzazz, joy & sharing that the equivalent book had & that was enough for me. This is not bragging; I'm just encouraging you to trust your own book-background, writer-skilled instincts & worry about the high-falutin' high-tech part later, if at all!

So, you can A, not look at any program — it isn't essential, or, B, see a few of the following:

The Encyclopedia: any multimedia brand will do. They'll show you the difference between using a book & using the multimedia version to achieve the same goals. You'll find some things you like. It's really impressive to see the Hindenburg & hear the actual radio report of its fiery crash, but I like to have several encyclopedia volumes open around me when I write.

Grandma & Me: art's the star here; kids click on various items to see them do charming things.

Sherlock Holmes: you'll see how the computer screen can be divided into various segments with several different things happening at once.

The Oregon Trail: One of my favorites! Like Sherlock Holmes, the "active" screen may be very small. Frankly, I'm glad I did NOT see this program before I began. I think I would have been intimidated, confused, technical-focused (instead of writing focused.) However, this mesh between "game" & "education" is very powerful & persuasive.

The Tales of Peter Rabbit: very simply shows you the pages on the screen, which you can "turn." Users click on a word to hear it spoken aloud; multilanguage.

Adult-oriented programs include **About Cows**, the **KGB-CIA Factbook** & others, all more boring (multimedia-wise) that the kids' programs noted above.

Frankly, I think one of the best things you can watch to get the "feel" of communicating via multimedia are the videos of the PBS series **The Civil War**, done by Ken Burns. Powerful words + strong visuals + an ever-changing kaleidoscope of "clicks," "buttons" & "links" that move from 1 place & topic to another so transparently & effectively, you forget that there *is no* video of the Civil War! (The programs on the **Donner Party** & on the building of the **Brooklyn Bridge** are also outstanding.)

Looking at any of these programs will let you see how you "get into" a program & begin this ebb & flow of interactivity, versus "turning the pages." However, I can tell you that right here, so you can get right to writing & look at stuff later!

NOTES

INTERESTED IN A SEMINAR BY CAROLE MARSH ON WRITING FOR MULTIMEDIA? CONTACT MICHELE YOTHER AT GALLOPADE PUBLISHING GROUP, 359 MILLEDGE AVE., SUITE 100, ATLANTA, GA 30312; CALL HER AT 404-577-5085; OR FAX HER AT 404-577-4881. CURRENT SCHEDULE:

September 1994, Louisville, KY
October 1994, Boston, MA
November 1994, San Antonio, TX
December 1994, Raleigh, NC
January 1995, Atlanta, GA

Chapter Nine:

Get With the Program:

Getting Into the Multimedia "Book"

The title page: Just like your book has a title page, your interactive multimedia program will have a Title Card. The only difference is, in a book, the reader knows to turn the page. In a program, they're going to look at that single computer screen & say "Huh, what?" unless you cue them what to do next. This can be a button that says BEGIN. An . A .

Or, it may automatically take them to another card after so many seconds.

WAIT!: Help, I'm already lost. I'm just the writer! This is page 1. Do I really have to do all this?

WRITER: This is the "new" challenge of interactive multimedia. Yes, you can leave all this to someone else who will mark up your copy with technical directions (similar to the stage directions in a play or script.) But you are creative & this is your baby. YOU know what you want to reader to do, hear, see, feel, understand.

So, my advice, is: when your new multimedia muse suggests an idea to you, add your instructions *in plain English.* There's nothing technical about that, but it'll be a real aid to the graphic artist or computer person who takes your manuscript the next step. If you don't know what to do, don't worry. But you — I guarantee! — are going to be a natural at this. So, when it occurs to you that you want your reader to "go to" X, just say so!

Copyright: Just like a book has copyright information, an interactive program has a card, screen, window or whatever that can automatically appear, be clicked on to appear, etc. to tell who's responsible for this mess or masterpiece, as the case may be. In my program, we had fun by letting the user click on **Carole Marsh** which linked them to a video of me telling how & why I came to do the program. I have to admit, it beat a boring old © symbol! To get with the program, you've got to give in to multimedia's potential — it's pretty

WOW!

NOW A WORD ABOUT HUMAN USER INTERFACE:

Remember when I said all those other multimedia books confused me? Well, it's because they threw terms like this out without explaining in plain English what they were talking about. HUI was one of the things they garbled the most, while at the same time telling me it was crucial to success. What is it? Remember when you used to stick your pj-clad kid on your lap & read it a bedtime story? "See the duck," you'd say & point to the picture of the duck. "This big long word is HELICOPTER," you'd say, pointing again. "Can you say helicopter?" This then, Mr. Roger's neighborhooders, is all HUI is! Helping the reader (Human) turn the page, or whatever (Use) the most logical (Interface) way. As you know, Macintosh won fame for being so good at this. Implied in its very simplicity was, "Hey, dummy, see the menu — pull it down!" Now, IBMers have their own little Windows on the HUI world. Don't let others make something easy hard for you! Just keep looking at that reader across your desk like you always did. Do what they need & that will be the right thing to do. Let some computer guru in her jammies figure out how to execute it in technicalese.

Wow! You already have 2 pages/screens done — what a good start you're off to! Now, follow me to the Table of Contents . . . or not?

Whoops — this is where multimedia can start to get messy, right from the start. BUT DON'T LET IT! I solved this "what next" problem by doing 2 things:

1. **I made a Table of Contents card.**

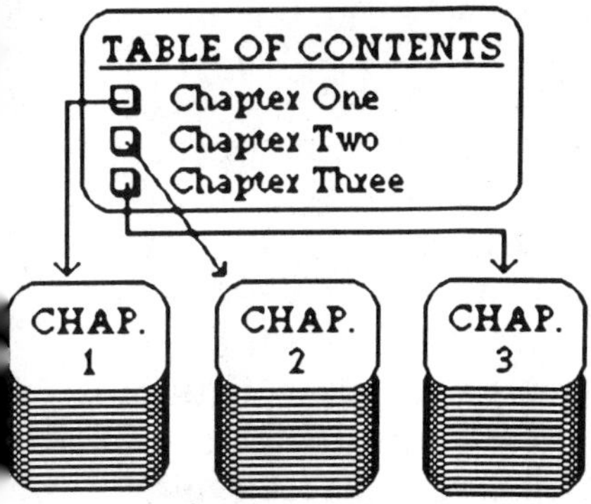

This has always been one of my sales pitches to the reader & I didn't want to do away with it. I wanted to use it just like a book does, to lead a reader into certain segments (chapters/stacks) of the program. So, each Table of Contents entry was a "hot" button. If the user clicked on it, he or she was immediately linked with the 1st card in that "chapter." You can do the same.

2. But hey, I <u>also</u> wanted users to know they could just go right to a "stack" of Biographies, for example. Or the teacher could assign students words to look up in the Glossary. Or, if they had been thru the program (or wanted to test their knowledge before beginning it), they could go right to the Pop Quiz.

This was my first startling departure from a strict "book" format to a more "multimedia" format. It felt very easy, very logical, very right. And therefore, I found, that just like I'd always done in my writing, I could create as I went along, letting the audience/topic/goal dictate what I did & when & how I did it.

So, I created a Card of Buttons (a Home Card) that represented my major focuses: history, geography, women, multicultures, etc. Try it!

Home Card? That's the main screen of buttons that tells the user what's in the program & (if they click on 1) takes them there. My programs have a Table of Contents <u>&</u> a Home Card. Yours can have whatever you want! Fortunately, there aren't many "rules" — & why should there be?! We writers are just now getting to flex our creative muscles in this new media. Just remember your Human User Interface (Keep It Simple, Stupid) & you'll be ok.

What do others do at this first of many anything-goes interactive junctions? In **Sherlock Holmes**, the format is a little board-gameish, with characters, clues, etc. to choose from. In **Where in the World is Carmen SanDiego?**, the "Home Card" caters more to buttons leading you to maps, research, etc. Every program is different, depending on the audience, content & purpose.

REMEMBER:

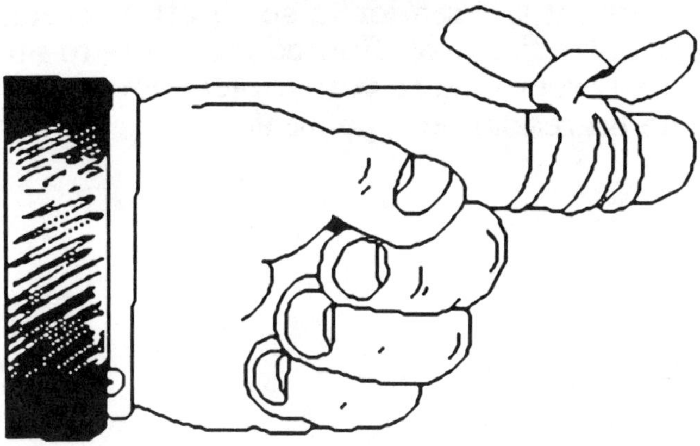

Interactive = you don't just read it, you explore it, may be able to talk to it (it may even talk back), write or draw in it, print cards out, take a score-keeping quiz, etc.

Multimedia = words + art, graphs, maps, charts & maybe photographs, animation, audio, & video.

Writers!

URGENT WRITING TIPS!: Write short! The goal of the program is to fill up lots of cards, lots of places for the user to go & explore. By the time you allow space for art, borders, buttons, etc., you'll find that short means real short! Yes, this feels quite tedious for "real writers," but the end result is much more attractive & communicative on the screen. The amount you write for a card is also determined by the size type you want the reader to see on the screen. See what size type you find comfortable to stare at on the screen before you subject your multimedia reader to type too tiny!

Chapter Ten:

The Storyline

Eureka! — here's a writing word you know. The only problem is that some multimedia programs have long, endless screens of copy (like legal briefs, for example) or are very piecemeal: a stack of this, a stack of that.

In my program, I wanted to have a backbone — a storyline, from which to branch off my "stacks" of information. So, to the 1st card linked to each Table of Contents listing, I linked other cards that were basically an intro to that "chapter" of information. Then, each of these cards had bold words, buttons or other "hot" items the user could click on to take them to additional information or visuals.

If you'd like to see a similar example, try **From Alice to Ocean**. This interactive multimedia program uses excerpts from the storyline of the book by the same name. Then you can click on map icons to follow a young woman's travels across the Australian outback or click on faces which come to life in video, telling about the rigors of the trip.

The Big Picture

I hope you're beginning to see the big picture! An interactive multimedia program can be anything you want it to be. Basically it's your book or story, divided into short segments in order to:

1. fit on a tiny computer screen, a segment at a time
2. link ancillary information to expand & enhance

In other words, where now you use Hints, Tips, *italicized material*, footnotes, sidebars, picture captions, etc. to explain more about the main body copy in your book, you can also do the very same thing in multimedia, only to a greater degree!

Where "author asides" are usually considered a no-no, I, the queen of "Hey, buddy" interruptions, can now give my reader all kinds of extras — without worrying whether they fit into the main stream of copy right at that point. This is a new freedom for writers used to linear copy. In multimedia, you can still write good, strong, tight copy — but also go off on wild tangents — right then while it's on your mind, while the reader may want to know, when the user expects it. This enables you to communicate in a new, stronger, high-impact, entertaining, intuitive way!

Writers!

URGENT ORGANIZATION TIP!: To keep your program "even," as far as a relative number of cards in each stack (if desired), do this: Use organization chart software (or just hand draw!) a chart of your stacks. As you write a card for a stack, put a mark in the appropriate box. That way, as you go along, you can see that your Science stack, for example, is being ignored, while your History stack is hogging all the information. In some multimedia programs, users not only like to explore at random, but also go through a complete stack, which is much more interesting if there're more than 1-2 cards there! You'll discover that you cater to certain subjects, but can quickly train yourself to perceive information as easily applicable to other categories. This way, when you finish your program, you're really finished & don't have to go back and fill-in uneven stacks.

Chapter Eleven:

There's Only One Problem!

Oops, you knew it was coming, didn't you? It is a problem, & it is a bad one, but it is solvable. What is it?

It's this: that suddenly, your copy is not completely <u>linear</u>. You can go off on a logical (or wild hair!) tangent every page, every paragraph, every phrase, every word, if you want to.

No, of course you're not trying to confuse your reader. It's just that now, you can stop & give examples, show, tell, elaborate. *And this is what multimedia was meant to do!*

The joy of multimedia is that if the user's interested in the history of quilts, he or she can devour that part of the program, completely avoiding the instructional portions. Even better, the user can create her own combination of logical or illogical trails through the information, because the writer has beckoned with all these enticing additions!

Yes, it's a lot like a book, only a reader might have to search long & hard for a 2nd reference to *trapunto,* for example, in a 1,000 page book (if the term does not appear in an index), while in a multimedia program, the writer's going to link such terms together so that someone interested in this form of quilting will discover references to it readily.

The problem is, this is a lot to keep in your head! "Oh," you say, "I'll just do index cards with arrows & spread them out around on the floor, so I can see what I'm doing." Or, "I'll use my flow chart software to keep up with all this."

Perhaps <u>you</u> can. But I found that being prepared, patient, & "linking" **as I went along**, so I could free my mind & go on, was the best method for me. It was intuitive & saved time. You'll have to figure out your own way. But the goal is to not get lost, so your reader won't get lost.

Other Considerations:

There are a few things that surprised me because they needed a "solution" in multimedia. For example:

Links: Having more than 1 link to a card may be logical, but you don't want *every* mention of Abraham Lincoln to link to his bio or the user will feel like they're on a dead end.

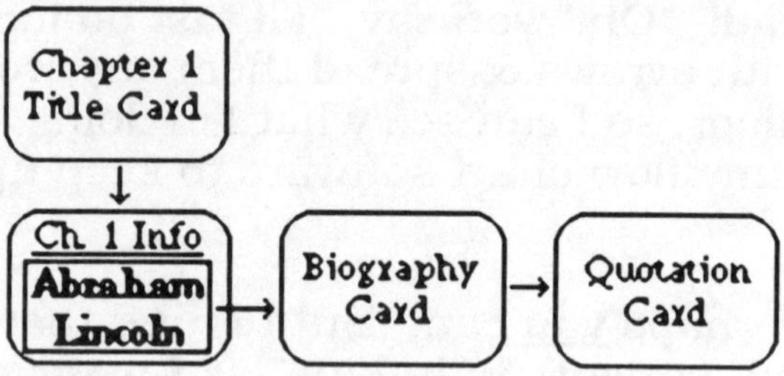

Returns: Users need a way to "get back" to the information they just left (which is now invisible to them!); this is accomplished by RETURN or ARROW buttons, but takes some thought on your part & indication to the computer person of where they go.

Loops: If a user has been reading through a stream of cards & takes a detour by clicking on a button to end up somewhere else in the program, you may want this to be in a multi-card loop, so they can explore new information, continue in this vein if they want to, or return to the spot they left off before you enticed them to look elsewhere. Again, just designate this at the end of that segment of your manuscript.

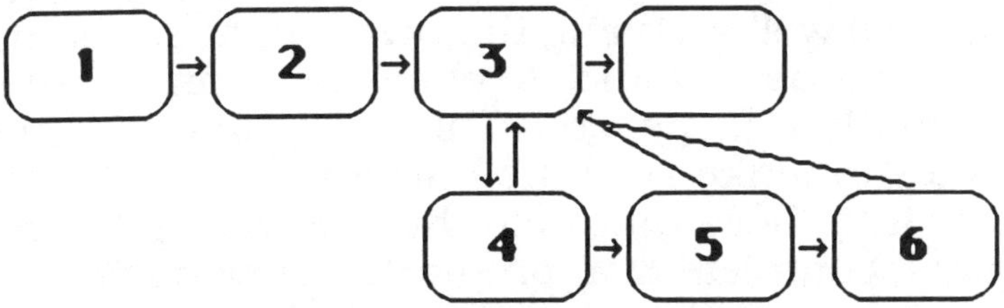

After the user leaves the original sequence on card 3 to explore a new sequence, they should be able to return to card 3 from any point along the detour sequence.

Continued information: Those little screens are not enough for some material; I found having some cards with a CONTINUE button solved this problem nicely & logically; other times, a scrolling card worked best.

Writers!

URGENT PROOFING TIP!: Spell-checking & proofing are doubly important in multimedia. Do the very best job you can on your copy of the program before it is translated into cards & stacks. It's not that it can't be corrected later, but it will be much easier to catch mistakes at this point in your writing. Once you get a program to proof, you'll want to go through each stack, as well as using the program at random, the way a user would, to check any continued information, loops, etc. This also will give you a chance to make sure the buttons, arrows & other interfaces that help the user navigate are logical, complete & appropriate. How do you know when you've gone through the whole program? Beats me! I never did figure that out!!

Chapter Twelve:

What Will My Manuscript Look Like?

Good question! Any way you want it to. However, it must be clear to you or the next person who must now turn what is still (technically) linear copy into *stacks* of *linked cards*. Fortunately, this can be best accomplished by plain English instructions before &/or after each card of information.

Man Overboard!

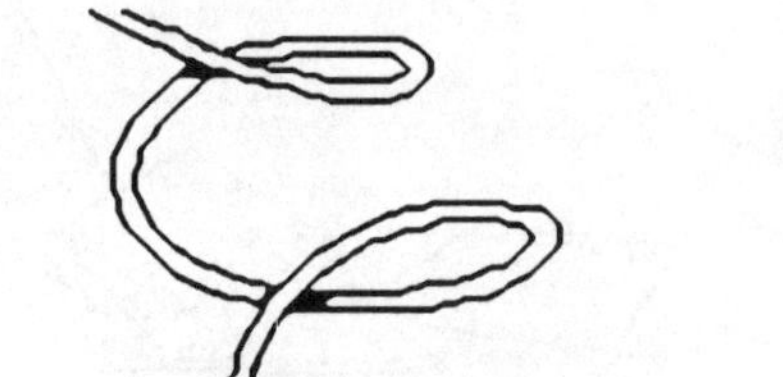

A word of caution: When I first started writing multimedia I was charmed into its endless opportunities for explanation. My 1st program was "The Mushroom on Mars Hill!": THE LOWELL OBSERVATORY & THE DISCOVERY OF PLUTO. As an example of my dilemma, I offer Percival Lowell, from Philadelphia. Well, it seemed logical to make **Philadelphia** a hot button so kids could click on the word & be linked to a card that told them where that city was, Pennsylvania, of course. Then I could bold **Pennsylvania** & take the user to information about that state. As you can see, before long, the program could have been retitled:

Lowell Observatory, the Discovery of Pluto, Where Every City & U. S. State Is & Everything About Everything Else in the World.

Fortunately, I saw the error of my ways fairly quickly before I sunk completely out of sight in what I came to call the Multimedia Mire. This is not what a program is meant to be. Use your audience & goal to keep you on track of what to put in, as well as what to leave out.

I mention this problem because it occurred again in other "big subject" titles like volcanoes & Indians. In some instances, linking Sioux City to its geographic explanation card is desirable, even necessary, while in other programs, it can get to be Bog Down Time very quickly, if you don't watch out.

Writers!

URGENT SURVIVAL TIP!: If you're like I *was* — an independent cuss of a writer who liked to work alone, be prepared to change your ways! Those of you who have worked in tandem with an illustrator, photographer, etc., will find your team experience an asset when it comes to working with a multimedia developer counterpart. My son, Michael, & I had it lucky; we'd been working together for 23 years. (Michael's only 22, but we started interacting well before he was born!) Because of both the *limitations* of multimedia and the *unlimitedness* of multimedia, you'll soon discover that your developer needs plenty of options, elbow room & leeway to alter or adjust your instructions. Squelch your ego & don't despair — these adjustments will almost always be an improvement. ("Michael," I said, "can't we put something for menu headings in our Cannibal example besides boring, old HELP, EDIT, etc.?" & the next Cannibal card I saw had APPETIZERS, ENTREES, & DESSERTS as the clever, creative answer to my question!) Once you & your developer learn to trust each other's instincts, intuition & creativity, you'll find that you won't have to struggle & sweat over a problem, but can share it & complement one another's skills & know-how. This will let you, writer, continue to write at light-speed (& thus make your million faster), depending on your developer to pick up the tune admirably in that gray area where it's hard to say where *multi* leaves off and *media* begins.

Chapter Thirteen:

Wouldn't All This Make More Sense If You Gave Me An Example?

That's just what I was thinking. So, here goes: Please note that I have gone a little wild with this juvenile title & the actual program is (a little bit) tamer!

The following is how I not only wrote my manuscript but also cued the computer programmer about what to link to what. We have transformed hundreds of pages of multimedia manuscript to actual interactive multimedia with nary a snafu. You can too! It's easy. Brevity, clarity & impact are key to being creative & communicative, but not confusing.

The Topic: CANNIBALS!

The Audience: 4th graders, who love stuff like this!

The Goal: to share a little of the fact & fiction behind this rarely-discussed subject, as an excuse to entice young readers into caring about history, geography, science, ethics & my other pet subjects like women, multicultures, literature & trivia.

Research: Oddly, the encyclopedia had a lot of info + my previous research on the Donner Party & other true-life accounts of contemporary cannibalism; cannibalism in art, music, movies; quotations; Columbus-era

Multimedia materials: cannibal art; video from movies; debate (where user has input); Donner Party photos; animation of a jungle/native sequence

Carole's Manuscript: Cannibal Program

CARD: Main Title Card
STACK: Main Storyline Stack
COPY: "In Good Taste": The Who, What, When, Where, Why & Why Not of **Cannibalism** by **Carole Marsh**
ART: Traditional cartoon of explorer-type in pot over fire in jungle; sound effects = drumbeats, jungle music/sounds
LINK: Bold words link to cards listed below

Michael's Final Card

CARD: Author's Note [starts STACK of cards by the same name; I will add to periodically throughout the program]
LINKS TO: **Carole Marsh** on card above
ART: either photo of me with apron, chef's hat, etc. OR video of same, me saying:

"I always worry if I should do a book I have in mind or not. Since I'm usually 'ahead of my time' on a subject, I often debate whether to write a book now, or later. This was certainly true when it came to cannibals! So, I watched for a sign. I was pondering aloud, when a co-worker spouted, "I was delivered by cannibals!" She went on to explain that her parents had been missionaries & she was delivered by the "Witch Doctor" of a tribe of cannibals the church worked with! I decided to do an interactive book & then this program. Actually, I guess you could say the idea just kept eating at me!"

Add TABLE BUTTON, so they can go to Table of Contents & start there;
Add HOME CARD BUTTON, so they can go see the Stacks of information available, if they want to start there

Appetizers Entrées Dessert Help
Cannibals
AUTHOR'S NOTES
STOP
PLAY

CARD: link this definition to the bold word **cannibalism** on the Title Card
STACK: goes in Glossary Stack

cannibalism *[can uh BAH liz em]:*
the eating of human flesh by human beings; also called anthropophagy

CARD: Table of Contents

COPY: Bone Appetite, The Dining Dilemma of the Donner Party, Hannibal the Cannibal, Who's for Lunch?, A Finger in Every Pot

ART: pots, bones, cooking utensils

(WRITERS, NOTE: HOW SIMPLE & CLEAN, PLAIN ENGLISH & INFORMAL YOUR MULTIMEDIA MANUSCRIPT CAN BE – NO MATTER HOW COMPLEX OR LONG YOUR PROGRAM!)

Appetizers Entrées Dessert Help

Cannibals

TABLE OF CONTENTS

Click on one of the chapter titles below to go to information about that topic.

① Bone Appetite

② The Dining Dilemma of the Donner Party

③ Hannibal the Cannibal

④ Who's for Lunch?

⑤ A Finger in Every Pot

CARD: Home Card; link each of the Button icons below to the 1st Card in their Stack

History Geography Biographies
Quotations Glossary
Activities Trivia Pop Quiz

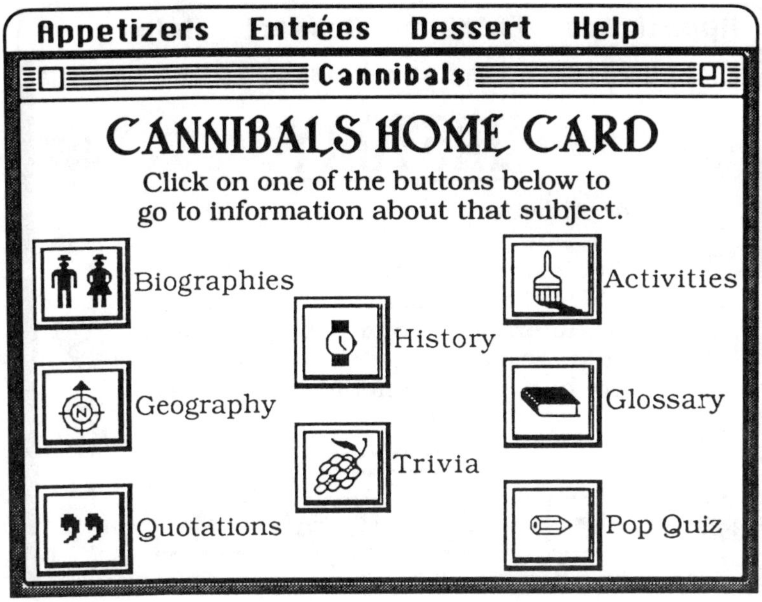

CARD: 1st card in History Stack
LINK: this card to the 1st entry in the Table of Contents
COPY: Bone Appetite!

In history, cannibalism was often considered a necessity for survival. Many **American Indian tribes** ate human flesh for several reasons, including severe hunger or ceremonial purposes.

SOUND EFFECTS: "natives are restless" music
Add Trivia BUTTON to bottom of card

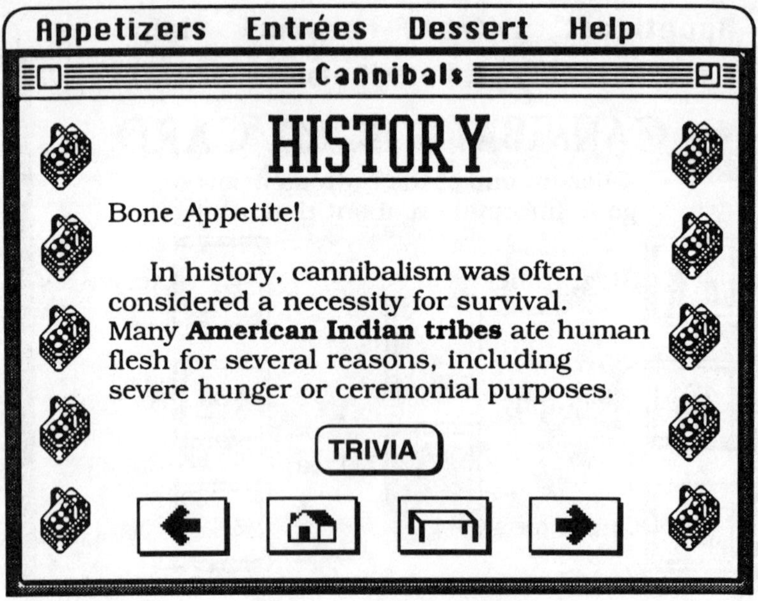

CARD: 1st card in Geography Stack; link to bold term on card above

COPY: American Indians known to participate in cannibalism included:

Algonquin Cree Fox Iroquois Micmac
Chippewa Kiowa Ceddo Sioux
Some California & Northwest Coast tribes

[Make each of the bold words above a separate card, linked in a loop with Arrows on the bottom of each card; link each of these cards to an illustration of that type of tribe]

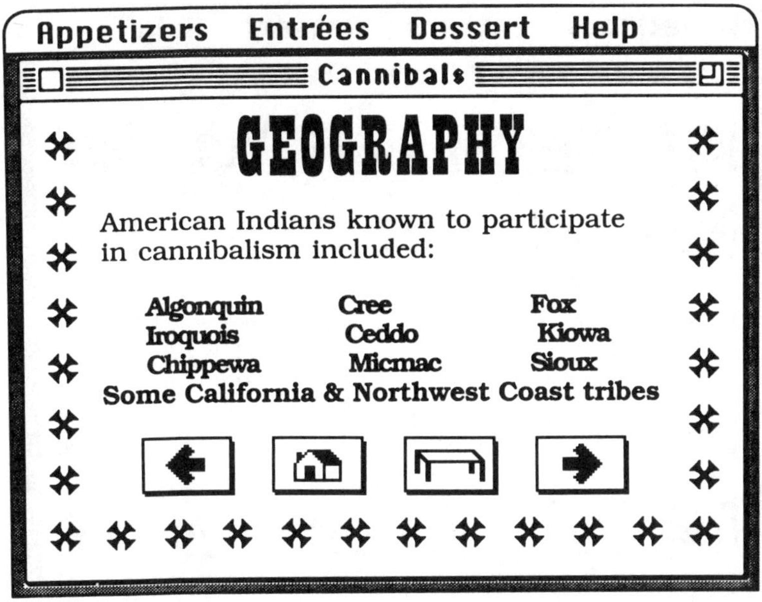

CARD: Trivia; link to the BUTTON on the card back above

COPY: What parts of people were most often eaten by cannibal tribes? [Put in a Pop Up answer box:] The heart, bone marrow & brains.

ADD a CONTINUE BUTTON to the bottom of the card

CONTINUED CARD; link to BUTTON above
COPY: Some prisoners of Indian tribes were tortured by being made to eat their own flesh!
ADD Science BUTTON to bottom of card

(WRITER: WE FOUND NO NEED TO NUMBER CARDS OR USE FORMAL, ARTIFICIAL OR ELABORATE TAGS. IN FACT, THIS SIMPLE PLAIN ENGLISH METHOD EVOLVED AFTER OTHER MORE CONFINING TRIES CONFUSED & FRUSTRATED ALL!)

Science CARD: link to BUTTON on card above

COPY: Some animals are "cannibalistic." They may eat their own young soon after they are born!

ART: Humorous cartoon of a puzzled baby on a plate at the kitchen table

Add QUOTATION BUTTON

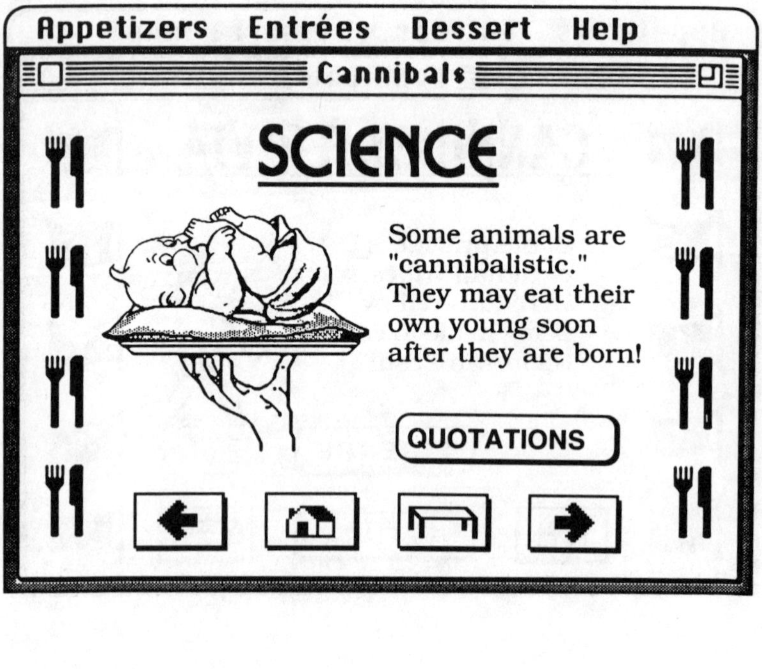

Quotation CARD; link to BUTTON above

COPY: "Never take no cut offs & hurry along as fast as you can." -- advice from pioneer **Virginia Reed**, member of the ill-fated **Donner Party**, 1896, caught in the winter snows & forced to resort to cannibalism to survive until the spring thaw.

Add ACTIVITY BUTTON

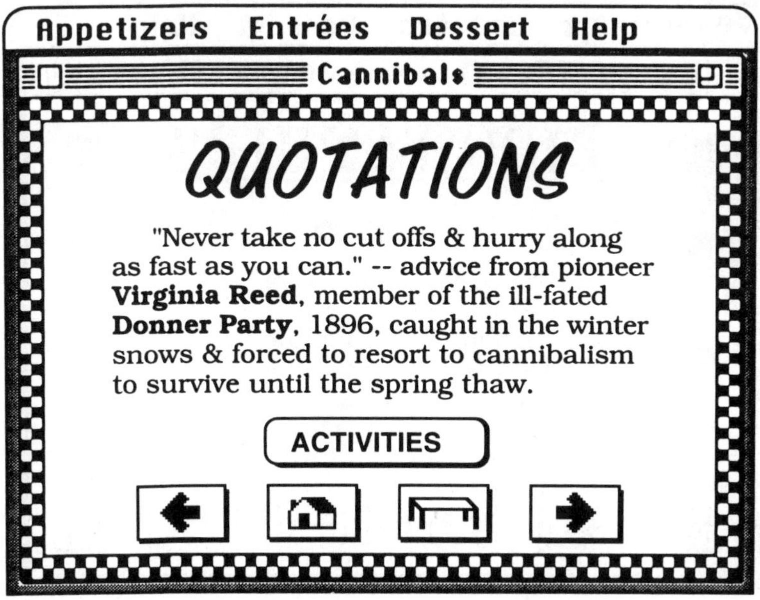

CARD: Bio; link to her bolded name on card above
STACK: Biography
COPY: Virginia Reed was one of the unfortunate members of the Donner Party which found itself debating whether or not to eat the dead & frozen family & friends in their party in order to survive the horrid winter.
ART: picture from historical archives
AUDIO: voice-over of her lamenting their situation

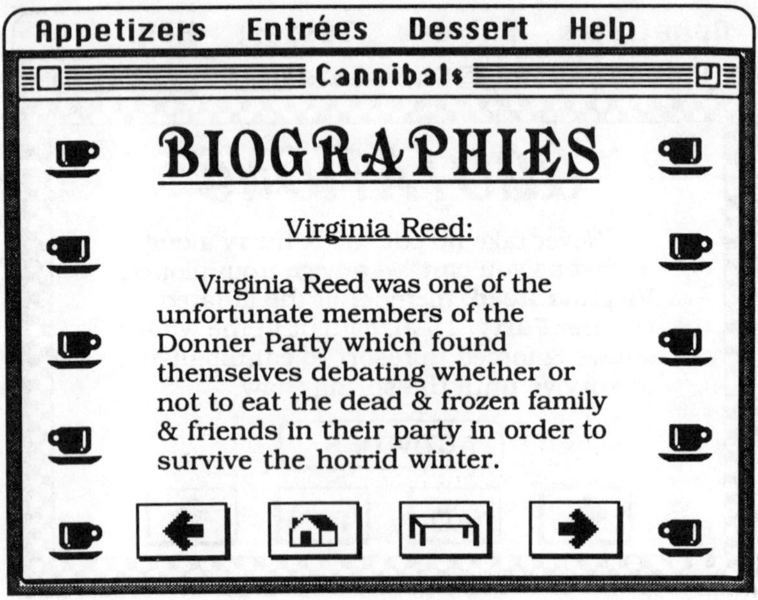

CARD: Activity; link to Activity Button on card back above

COPY: The Case for Cannibalism

LINK: to video clip of narrator setting the stage for a debate among air crash survivors [mock scene]

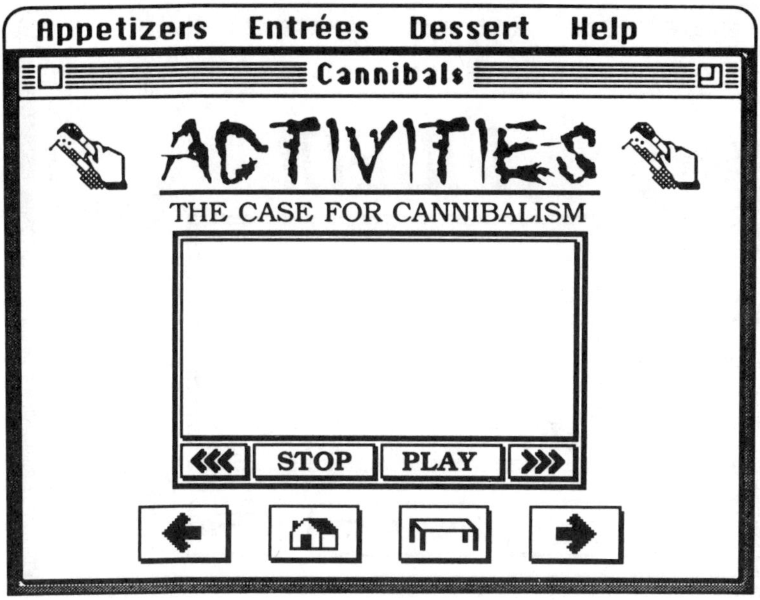

VIDEO: "Think!: We always make fun of cannibalism & picture "the natives" with a perplexed explorer in a pot. But what if <u>you</u> were faced with a life or death situation where eating the dead was the only means of survival?"

ADD POP QUIZ BUTTON

CARD: Pop Quiz
STACK: Pop Quiz
COPY: This is a self-testing debate to see how you feel about cannibalism.
LINKS: Questions go on individual cards LINKED to one another in a loop.

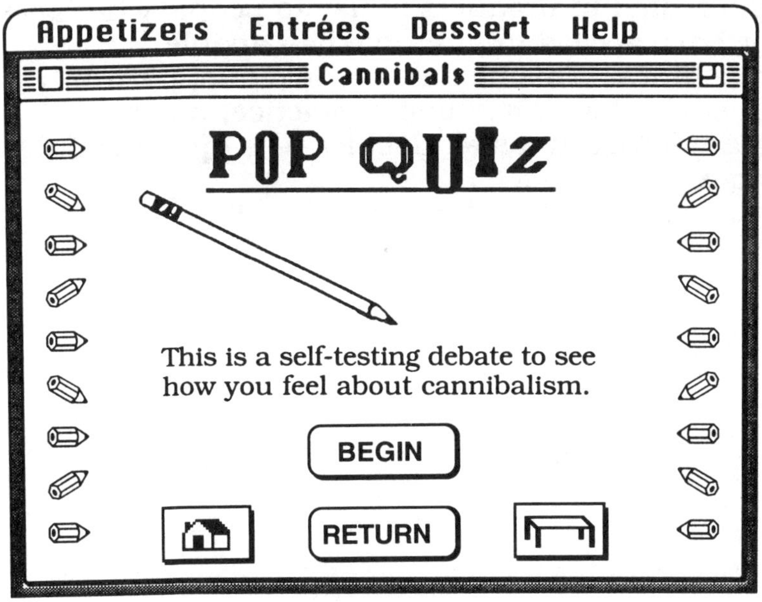

NOTES

One of the exciting aspects of writing for multimedia is that it offers job opportunities of global proportions! Early reviews of this book were picked up by newspapers around the world. Many of the articles appeared in "Career" columns. The installed-base of multimedia & CD-ROM players is worldwide. Indeed, some countries, which were "behind the times" (technologically), used new funds to invest in the most cutting-edge equipment available. Publishers from around the world are getting involved in multimedia. I believe they will be interested in products of use to people who have, or have access to, multimedia-capable machines. This means the field of opportunity in education, government, science, medicine & many other areas — globally — is open to you *now*.

Chapter Fourteen:

Is That All There Is?

As you can see, this is a very simple version, but a very complete one. Even the addition of more copy, art, buttons or links does not make it more complex or confusing IF you stay organized & communicate clearly.

Some multimedia programs keep lots of Buttons on the screen at the same time. Others have more than 1 card or window open at the same time.

There are no rules! This was my way; you can make up your own way. The key questions are:

✔ **Am I getting my program off to an inviting & logical start?**

✔ **Does the user know where to go, what to do next?**

✔ **Does the information have a logical flow?**

✔ **Are links logical? Do they expand on the previous information. Do they often offer little "surprises" so that they aren't so predictable?**

✔ **Can each card stand alone in case the user reads it out of sequence from my planned flow?**

✔ **Have I watched pronouns & not used "it" (for example) to refer to a word on an unseen card?**

✔ **Have I been careful not to put so much information on a card that there's no room for borders, art, buttons, etc.?**

✔ **Have I been careful not to <u>tell</u> what visuals <u>show</u>; have I also explained what visuals the user is seeing?**

✔ **Does each card have a way for the user to return to the card they previously left, if they want to?** (Arrow Buttons do this.)

✔ **Are cards interesting, informative, inviting & involving?**

✔ **Have I tried to make each card as interactive as possible; have I also been careful not to load a card with so many choices that the user is confused, bored or bogged down?**

NOTES

As a writer you might ask, "Will my multimedia titles be sold at the same place my books are now?" The answer seems to be: "Probably." For a long time, booksellers seemed to balk at the idea of carrying a medium (CD-ROMS) that appeared to be contributing to the so-called death of the book. However, recent U. S. & international book shows have found multimedia booths & seminars packed by booksellers interested in handling the new media. I believe that in the near future you'll see your multimedia products in direct marketing catalogs, bookstores, computer software outlets, audio/video chains, specialty retail stores, public & school libraries, & everywhere else that books are commonly sold today.

Chapter Fifteen:

Human In-Your-Face Design!

As you can see, your program is like a direct dialog between you & your reader! Therefore, if you can put yourself in the user's place, you can "plug in" their questions, wonderings, want-to-know-nexts as you go along, only instead of doing it in a long linear line or a horizontal flip chart booklet, you knit nice little links & loops to help them skip, skim & scour the information that most interests them.

Interactivity Tips!

It may take you awhile to get the hang of interactivity. As writers, we're often used to just adding more words to continue our explanation. But with multimedia, you can do some or all of the following, if you like: (These are just a few examples!)

Have boxes, cards, screens, etc. where users can write their own information

- Let the user circle words in a Word Search

- Let the user fill-in-the-blanks

- Let the user complete a matching activity

- Let the user draw a picture

- Let the user participate in a quiz & get an audio response depending on the answer.

The Game Aspect

While I've focused on a straight-forward version of an interactive multimedia program, you can make yours more of a game with some score-keeping mechanism.

In **Oregon Trail**, users match wits against enemies & elements by selecting a role to play, receiving funds to purchase supplies, choosing their own path — & suffering the consequences of each decision — learning history & geography along the way, with a few laughs thrown in for good measure.

(I kept drowning in the river, dadgummit.)

NOTES

Is Content King?

Here are just a few quotes from current multimedia publications touting the importance of "content":

"What is in short supply . . . people with creative ideas to develop 'killer' content."

[Interactive multimedia] "Discs will sell because of the content, not the interactivity."

"Just like with books, people want multimedia programs on subjects of interest to them, they want to learn, to think, to feel, not navigate mindlessly through some graphic arts wasteland."

Chapter Sixteen:

The Rest of the Story

The Rest of the Story: Part I

ANYTHING you can create & communicate in writing, you can try. Unless you are the "next person" in the multimedia program development stage, someone else will have to figure out "how" to accomplish your wishes. Often, they'll have impressive ideas of how to add interactive pizzazz to your creation. Other times, they may ask you to eliminate or tame something because of technical limitations or lack of sufficient memory.

The Rest of the Story: Part II

If YOU are the person who'll also transfer your manuscript into a multimedia "authoring program," you'll now have a head start on being able to use a simple program, such as Hypercard. *(My programs were done in Supercard on a Macintosh LC jazzed up with extra memory by my son who self-taught himself as he went along.)*

There are other more complex & expensive programs for Macintosh, DOS, Unix & other formats. You will want to use an authoring program (software) that will let your finished program run on the platforms (hardware) marketed to. This means you may do a program in Macintosh, then also translate it into Windows, for example.

Soon, there should be simple, object-oriented authoring programs that let you produce a product that will run on most any platform, the way audio compact disks play in any player.

The Rest of the Story: Part III

Whoever "completes" your multimedia program will do some or all of the following:

- **Put each segment of information on a separate card.**
- **Designate these cards for a particular Stack.**
- **Link Cards and/or Stacks together as you have designated.**
- **Link Animation, Sound Effects, Photos, Video, etc. as you have specified.**

Note: All this is easier than it sounds for a simple program. In Hypercard or Supercard, for example, a Card is just a blank screen. Merely by using the Menu, you can make Dialog Boxes appear that ask you what you want to link that card to. As I said earlier, you can buy or copy pre-scripted Buttons. It's even easy to script your own simple buttons in plain English. More complex programs, requiring actual programming, are more difficult for the computer-technician, but you can write for such programs the same way.

There are programs such as **Macromedia Director**, which let you group all your "stuff" into a single document.

Whichever software application is used, eventually everything gets put in place & the program should be tested. Watch others use it. There will be changes to make & you will learn greatly from actual user input.

Once the program is tested, it can be finalized by *compressing* the document so that it takes up as little memory space as possible, important if it will be sold on diskettes.

If the program will be on a CD-ROM, it will be Pre-Mastered, either by a CD-ROM plant or a "One-Off" machine in-house or at a service bureau. After the pre-master is tested, a Master is made & final CDs are Replicated or pressed.

NOTES

CHECKLIST OF NEW MEDIA WRITING OPPORTUNITIES!:

- ❑ Electronic books, catalogs & sales brochures
- ❑ Self-running information kiosks & demos
- ❑ Interactive business presentations
- ❑ Animated presentations
- ❑ Executive Information Systems (EIS)
- ❑ Corporate portfolios
- ❑ CD-ROMs for adults or children
- ❑ Self-paced learning
- ❑ Computer-based training
- ❑ Art & entertainment games

Chapter Seventeen:

Let's Talk About That Million!

As a publisher, after years of paying big bucks for expenses such as typesetting, paste up & art, printing & binding, I was really excited by the prospect of a skinny slip of plastic that could easily be copied, perhaps even "on demand"! No matter what the price, it would change my publishing economics dynamically! And this is true.

However, the upfront costs of a larger & more powerful color computer, new software, training, additional fees for photos, video, animation, etc., seem to have offset any savings so that whether it's a book, diskette or CD-ROM, my costs seem pretty much the same, just switcherooed from the end to the beginning.

But, you the writer, can get in on all this action for virtually NO MORE MONEY! "Content" — quality, accurate, informative, emotional words -- is what's required of you. Even if you write non-fiction, short stories, poetry, cookbooks, or anything else LIKE YOU'VE ALWAYS WRITTEN IT, you can take this book & examples & develop a creative interactive multimedia program!

Other opportunities include: interactive multimedia manuals, training programs, catalogs, documentation & much more.

Contracts

If you're a published author, you may have already inadvertently given away some multimedia rights. Don't worry — who coulda known? But from this point on, all writers should read the fine print & retain, or sell for an appropriate fee, rights to conversion of your manuscript to interactive, multimedia or other electronic formats.

Copyright Protection

There's no difference in how you protect your written multimedia program than any other manuscript you write. However, once the program has other artists' pictures, photos, animation & video, it becomes a unique animal that stands on its own. The lawyers will make the first million!

And what happens when someone sees your bio of Bill Clinton on a screen with no immediate designation of ©You? Unfortunately, some folks, with no background in writing, think it's ok to copy this. Obviously, we disagree, & multimedia lawyer types are hashing all this out right now.

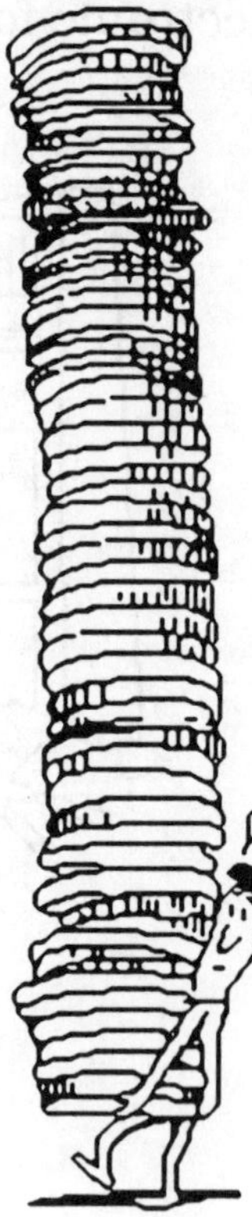

Be cautious. Be realistic. But also help set newcomers straight & strive for ongoing copyright protection for writers who've fought hard for the protections we have today & expect for tomorrow's electronic world.

Payment

Good question, but who knows? As usual, it's make the best deal you can. I think it's fair to assume the same position you would take if it were a book contract. However, this seems to be a market with lots of middlepeople. It's also very expensive for publishers to get involved in all this new equipment & training. Wholesalers & distributors want very deep discounts. So get in on the action, but be willing to wheel & deal with new percentages. In multimedia, words only make up part of the program. Also, don't sell too much! One of my mistakes was trying to write gigantic programs just because a CD-ROM would hold it all. But a CD-ROM will also hold a whole lot of smaller programs. So, do just like you would a book or article: pitch the best subject & slant to the best audience. Write what it takes, then stop. Let the rest of the space be taken up with all the new visuals & leave plenty of space for running the thing. After all, do you really care if you make that million a few hundred or thousand dollars at a time? Small, short programs may be the best way to get started, allow you plenty of learning curve, be less frustrating — it is brain-taxing, I promise — & let you see a final program in print (so to speak) so you can see what you would do differently the next time, based on user feedback.

NOTES

MULTIMEDIA SKILLS FOR HIRE!

- ❑ New title development
- ❑ Research (including of graphics, audio, video)
- ❑ Program design
- ❑ Writing
- ❑ Editing
- ❑ Interactive enhancements
- ❑ Art production
- ❑ Photography
- ❑ Graphic art production
- ❑ Video making & editing
- ❑ User interface design
- ❑ Program testing, checking
- ❑ Database management

Chapter Eighteen:

What you will learn from your 1st program!

It takes a program or 2, or 8 to get accustomed to this new way of writing, this way that is the same, but different. You'll discover it certainly uncovers any sloppy writing habits you may have developed over the years that can get buried in a couple of hundred pages of copy, but stand out like a sore thumb on a single in-your-face multimedia card.

You'll learn how to think <u>interactively</u>; ideas you might once automatically have put into words, you'll begin to visualize in more dramatic ways.

Your association with your audience will evolve differently. You'll establish more of a dialog, where you're communicating *with* them, instead of *to* them, & they back with you.

You'll learn how to best communicate your creative concepts to the next person in the development process, whether graphic artist or computer programmer. You may discover some exciting team spirit here & your ideas enlarged & enhanced.

You may also find that you like multi-media just fine & look forward to its future, whether that's the inclusion of smell, touch, 3-dimensions or whatever amazing thing that a book, much as we love it, just can't do!

NOTES

Back to School!

1. If you want to see where your multimedia products might appear, check out your local school system. You might be surprised to discover how high-tech they have gone with "teaching walls," networked multimedia stations & more.

2. Want to learn more about how to multimedia? The Savannah School of Art & Design in Savannah, Georgia offers a degree in multimedia. Georgia Tech in Atlanta now has a multimedia program in place. San Francisco State University is developing 3 CD-ROMs to teach multimedia at the college level; SFS has the largest multimedia training center in the country. Arizona State University offers a college course, "Instructional Media Design" on CD-ROM; students will send assignments over the Internet.

Part III:

MultiHelp

Chapter Nineteen:

Recommended Products

This is strictly a list of products I've used or researched & I recommend them ONLY because I believe them to be *easy* — & fast & easy is our primary criteria for selecting such items! Some products are listed that we're just now using for conversion of our multimedia disks into CD-ROM format, but our research has shown that these seem to meet our fast & easy objective + have bugs worked out & offer good technical support.

MULTIMEDIA WRITING COMPUTER:

Obviously I'm a Macintosh fan! But I do believe using either Macintosh (any model that uses System 7 will be ok for writing) OR a DOS computer with Windows is best. Why? Because the very object-oriented, menu-driven, point & click Human User Interface designs incorporated exemplify what you're trying to accomplish. Multimedia is supposed to be intuitive, foolproof, easy, fun, fast, useful. Don't you hate to read the manual? Well, multimedia users just want to interact; if they wanted to read, they'd buy a book. A color computer is not critical for writing a multimedia program. Using a color monitor, though, helps you begin to see & think more visually, including about colors, & may help you in being more creative in your ideas for the program.

MULTIMEDIA WRITING SOFTWARE:

I use **Write Now**, again, because it's fast & easy. As far as I know, any word processing program will work just fine. If you use Macintosh, I'd go ahead & try to switch to System 7 (if you haven't), so things will be as compatible with the next steps as possible. You could write your program right into Hypercard, Supercard or another basic authoring program. However, I think it's hard enough to CREATE & WRITE the program, without worrying about even a smidgen of additional computer organization. Whatever you do, be sure & do thorough copy-editing & spell-checking before you hand-off the program. It's much easier & faster to correct errors here than later on when the same word may be misspelled on 20 cards!

MULTIMEDIA AUTHORING SOFTWARE:

There's a wide range of authoring software; some is very difficult & expensive. There's some proprietary authoring software out there that companies are beginning to let developers use to write their programs in, either by buying the software or on a fee basis. For your first program, Hypercard or Supercard may work just fine. With these programs, you can create Cards, Buttons, Links, & add Interactivity, such as drawing, typing, add simple Sound Effects, artwork, & color slides. If you are a DOS person, try a program called, GRASP, or Hyperties. But remember, you DO NOT need an "authoring" program to write multimedia.

MULTIMEDIA EQUIPMENT:

If you want to carry your written program to the next step, you'll need all the RAM & hard drive memory you can get! No, I don't mean that you necessarily need the latest PowerMac or Power PC, but multimedia application programs take up a lot of space & need plenty of elbow room to run. A program that runs 100 pages on your writing computer — & will fit on a single floppy disk — will expand exponentially when color, art, photos, etc. are added. This work must be done in an *uncompressed* form & can only be compressed when you're finished.

We took an intermediate step & used a souped-up Macintosh LC (low-end of the line) to do the authoring, add art, develop the animation, sound effects & videos. Then when we had all the pieces together, we had to give in & step up our computer & memory to assemble it all. But, doing it this way saved us 1 year's worth of computer payments & the price on the machine we wanted went down in the meantime!

Also, there are service bureaus that can do "everything else" for you. You'll have to decide how deep you want to participate in & finance your multimedia role. If you're doing a project on assignment, then the publisher should be able to take your writing on diskette & go from there. If you have a more informal association, such as I had with my son, your partner will certainly need a hard copy of your writing as well as a disk. Also, be prepared for plenty of questions. They may be a multimedia expert, but know little about your program subject.

NOTE: Another reason for lots of hard disk space, even as a writer, is this: It won't take you long to figure out that if you're going to do a number of multimedia programs, there's no reason for you to have to look up "paleontologist" & define it more than once. You'll want to build a "library" of Cards of information that you can just copy & plug into your subsequent programs as needed. Likewise, by the time art & color are added to these Cards, you or the computer person will want to save these so they need not be redone for each program. Even after a single program, we discovered many items, ranging from card borders to pre-colorized art to definitions that we could reuse, quickening the pace of our development & saving money.

MULTIMEDIA SOFTWARE:

A program like **Macromedia Director** lets you assemble all the parts of your program into 1 document. I consider the computer person a real orchestrator at this point who can certainly make a program sing! Software such as **Video Spigot** lets you pour video into your computer so that you can edit it for inclusion in a multimedia program. **Video Toaster** lets you add special effects like a movie camera does when switching from 1 scene (Card) to another. There are all kinds of individual programs for everything from type manipulation to sound effects creation to 3-D animation. When completed, software such as **Stuffit** will compress your program as a stand-alone application so that it appears on the user's screen as a single icon which they click on to open the program. Little will they know all the steps that came before to create even a simple program!

MULTIMEDIA PROGRAMMING:

You can create a simple, interactive multimedia program without a computer programmer or doing any programming. They (or you) may be able to figure out how to do simple, plain English scripting; there are also many pre-scripted items you can buy. But as you might imagine, there's simple & there's complex. You aren't going to be able to do every wild & crazy thing you envision without programming assistance. If you're working with a publisher, they'll provide that. But if you, or you & a partner, want to complete a simple, colorful, very attractive, very interactive program — you can do it without being a bona fide computer programmer.

CD-ROM:

Lots of developers are doing interactive multimedia on diskettes that work either with Macintosh or Windows-based computers. Why? Because that's what most customers have to use right now. There're also a lot of CD-ROMs out there that will run on virtually any CD-ROM player, no matter what computer it's hooked up to. What the user sees on the screen is really no different. The difference is that a CD-ROM holds so very, very, *very* much more material. As the base of CD-ROM players grows, most folks believe this will be the most common format programs come in because of how much they can hold & because they will be compatible with most equipment. Right now, a single CD may hold multiple versions of a program, or hold a number of completely different programs which are "unlocked" as the purchaser buys them.

MULTIMEDIA STORAGE:

One encouraging thing to keep in mind is that basically all the "pieces" of a program, from your writing to a sound bite, to a slide, a piece of art, or even a video are expressed on the computer screen as individual documents. This means that programs such as Kodak's **Shoebox** or **Fetch** & others, will come in very handy to store an assortment of multimedia program materials which you can call up, copy & paste to use again.

As a writer, you may want to begin to think about how you'll store your written programs so that you can access the bits & pieces you want to use again. If you have a search program such as **Sonar** (which searches very quickly across unopened documents), just keeping the final programs may satisfy you. If you're an organization freak like me, you might want to have various documents & folders of like items, such as glossary definitions, biographies, quotations, etc. — whatever the type of material you write.

Software Buyers!

URGENT PURCHASING TIP!:
Remember, you may have to pay a royalty each time some programs are used that help make your program work. Be sure & check on this *before* you purchase an application program.

NOTES

MY ADVICE:

Early orderers of this book surprised me! You are from everywhere in the world. You may be a writer struggling to see where your skills mesh with the more graphical end of the multimedia world. Or, you may be a photographer, videographer, graphic artist eager to learn to write text to accompany your work. Your expertise may be in computer programming. Or maybe your corporation or school is pushing you into the development of interactive electronic learning. Some of you are publishers trying to educate writers in new methods. Others are developers trying to manage creative types. Whatever position you come from, try to compartmentalize your skills. If this is writing, first get it "up to speed" for multimedia. You may find that the "rest of the story" is farmed out to pros in other areas, leaving you more time to write new programs. Or you may decide that you want to add additional multimedia expertise to your bag of skills. If so, go slow. Learn not only the skill, but exactly what format it must be in to be usable in multimedia. This may be digital, instead of analog, multi-platform instead of single, for examples. In other words, there are new aspects to take into consideration for each piece of the multimedia package.

Chapter Twenty:

Appendix

The Complete Sound Effects Library
by Sony Music Special Products
A set of 10 Compact Disks; available from most compact disk dealers.
I have a printed list of the sound effects included so that I can "spec" ones & know the computer developer actually has access to them.

The WPA Film Library
5525 W. 159th St.
Oak Forest, IL 60452
Can send you a video of historical clips, as well as humor/silly & all types of subjects, so that you can see the kinds of segments you can "spec" for your program at about $1.00 per *second* !

Meckler Publishing
11 Ferry Lane West
Westport, CT 06880
Get on their mailing list for information about multimedia & CD-ROM directories, magazines & exhibits!

Apple CD-ROM Handbook: A Guide to Planning, Creating & Producing a CD-ROM
by Apple Computer, Inc.
Published by Addison Wesley
A useful book to see everything from start-to-finish. (But does <u>not</u> tell you how to write!)

Chapter Twenty-One:

You Were Made for Multimedia!

There is indeed a million to be made in multimedia! But of just as much value: how lucky we are as writers to live in a time when we can participate in a whole new era of writing & creativity! Gutenberg may be rolling in his grave, but I think he would surely "CD light" & I hope you do too!

You were made for multimedia! Go for it! *Today!!*

INTERACTIVE MULTIMEDIA ASSOCIATION,
3 Church Circle, Suite 800,
Annapolis, MD 21401-1933
410-626-1380
Has newsletters, a directory, seminars.

CD-ROM PROFESSIONAL MAGAZINE,
462 Danbury Rd
Wilton, CT 06897-2126
call 800-248-8466 to subscribe.
Excellent publication on all facets of multimedia!

CD-ROM WORLD MAGAZINE,
11 Ferry Lane West
Westport, CT 06880-9760
call 1-800-MECKLER to subscribe.
Reader-friendly publication; excellent for newcomers to market.

Write **DATAWARE** Technologies for a free Guide to CD-ROM & Multimedia Publishing,
222 Third St., Ste. 3300
Cambridge MA 02142.

WIRED
544 2nd Street
San Francisco, CA 94107
Check your newsstand for this monthly marvel of info on what's next in multimedia's future!

MULTIMEDIA SCHOOLS,
"A Practical Journal of Multimedia,
CD-ROM, Online & Internet in K-12"
Subscriptions: $38 per year/USA & Canada,
$51/Mexico, $60, foreign airmail.
Write 462 Danbury Rd., Wilton, CT 06897.
Excellent source of information for writers of educational multimedia.

MULTIMEDIA WORLD MAGAZINE
Write 501 Second St., #110,
San Francisco, CA 94107.
Published monthly; subscriptions run $14.97 per year.

MAC HOME JOURNAL
544 Second St., San Francisco, CA 94107.
Published monthly; subscriptions $19.95 per year.

About the Author

Carole Marsh founded **Gallopade!, The World's Largest Publishing Company** in 1979. A former Communicator of the Year among Fortune 500 companies & winner of many awards for her writing & photography, she transformed her public relations/corporate communications agency (Marsh Media Methods) into an international self-publishing operation.

Starting with a single title, Carole has more than 2,500 books in print, published on-demand for each day's orders which come from extensive direct marketing campaigns around the U. S., Canada & the world. For a number of years, her books were offered not only in paperback & hardcover, but on computer disk, which was very popular.

In 1993, Marsh established **Carole Marsh Family Interactive Multimedia & CD-ROM** & is now in the process of creating original programs as well as converting many of her books into interactive multimedia. Marsh also created WPUN-FM & WPUN-TV to create audio & video for multimedia & has established Channel A^+ in anticipation of marketing her programs directly to consumers over the new fiber optic networks.

This family operation, including Carole's daughter Michele Yother (president), husband Bob Longmeyer (videographer), & son Michael Marsh (multimedia developer), is based in 3 virtual offices in 2 states, North Carolina & Georgia.

For a copy of Gallopade's LIFEWRITE & PROPUB or HOW TO MAKE A MILLION titles, or to order Interactive Multimedia Programs, write to 359 Milledge Ave., Suite 100, Atlanta, GA 30312 or call 1-800-536-2GET.

INDEX